London

a guide to places of Spiritual interest

SPIRIT OF BRITAIN

Series introduction

The British have never been keen on organized religion; attendance at public worship has always been low, and today barely one person in twenty regularly goes to a service. Yet the people of this island have always had a passion for religious buildings, and have erected some of the finest in the world. And today more people than ever visit them — usually at times when they can wander round undisturbed by any priests or preachers. British spirituality is informal and personal.

This series is a guide to the places of greatest spiritual interest in Britain. And each book suggests tours — pilgrimages — around a particular region of the country.

If Geoffrey Chaucer, writing several centuries ago, is to be believed, pilgrims in Britain have always enjoyed themselves, even as they purified their souls. May you continue that tradition.

Introduction

London has been the capital city of England for two millennia; and two pilgrimages are suggested. The first, starting at St Paul's cathedral, centers on the ancient area of the city founded by the Romans, and remains the financial heart of the country. The second, starting at Westminster abbey, covers places that, until medieval times and later, were separate towns and villages, but now include the most fashionable residential and shopping areas of Britain.

Each pilgrimage may take a weekend or three days. You can, of course, add all the conventional tourist attractions to your itinerary — you will go past most of them — so your trip will take longer. Or you can simply do parts of the pilgrimages on occasional days. Driving round London is slow, and involves a ceaseless hunt for parking spaces. Directions are given for going round on foot, with occasional journeys on an underground train (subway). A good street map is vital.

CONTENTS

ROUTE ONE

Directions 4
St Paul's Cathedral 6
St Mary Le Bow 8
The Temple of Mithras 10
St Magnus the Martyr 12
Southwark Cathedral 14
Spanish and Portuguese Synagogue 16
East London Central Mosque 18
Jamme Masjid Mosque 20
John Wesley's House and Museum 22
St John's Church and Gate 24
City Temple 26
St Bride's Church 28
Dr Johnson's House 30
Temple Church 32

ROUTE TWO

Directions 34
Westminster Abbey 36
Westminster Chapel 38
Westminster Cathedral 40
Brompton Oratory 42
Holy Trinity, Brompton 44
Chelsea Old Church 46
Peace Pagoda 48
Buddhapadipa Temple 50
St Paul's Church 52
Pet Cemetry 54
Rada Krishna Temple 56
Swaminarayan Hindu Temple 58
London Central Mosque 60
St Jame's Church 62

ROUTE ONE

East London

 Start at **St Paul's**.

Go along Cheapside to **St Mary-le-Bow** which is on the right.

Continue along Cheapside, and turn right into Queen Street. Then turn left onto Queen Victoria St. On the right is the **Temple of Mithras**.

Continue to the junction where the Bank of England stands, and turn right into King William Street. Go past the Monument station, turn left along Monument Street, and right down Fish Street Hill. Opposite the end of Fish Street Hill, on Lower Thames Street, is **St Magnus the Martyr**.

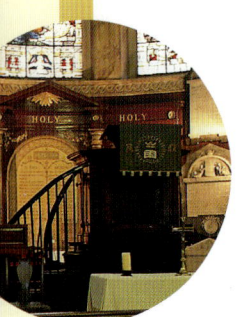   

Turn right along Lower Thames Street, and cross London Bridge. At the far side on the right are steps leading down to **Southwark Cathedral**.

Go back across London Bridge and along King William Street. At the Monument Station fork right up Gracechurch Street. This becomes Bishopsgate. Turn right into Camomile Street, and then becomes Bevis Mark. On the right, just beyond Bury Street, is the **Spanish and Portugese Synagogue**.

Continue along Bevis Marks, which becomes Dukes Place. Fork left into Aldgate High Street, which becomes Whitechapel High Street, which in turn becomes Whitechapel Road. On the right, beyond Plumbers Row, is the **East London Central Mosque**.

Return down Whitechapel Road, and turn right at Osborn Street. This become Brick

ROUTE ONE

Lane. On the left, on the corner of Fournier Street, is the **Jamme Masjid Mosque**, which was originally the New French Church.

Go along Fournier Street, cross Commercial Street into Brushfield Street. Turn left into Bishopsgate, and right along Liverpool Street. At the end turn left and then right into Finsbury Circus. Turn right into Moorgate, which becomes City Road. On the right, just after Epworth Street, is **John Wesley's House and Church**.

Continue up City Road to a major junction, and turn left into Old Street, which becomes Clerkenwell Road. After St Bartholomew's Hospital and St John Street, turn right into St. John's Square. On your right are the gates, through which is visible the garden built on the ruins of St John's Church. Turn back across Clerkenwell Road into St John's Lane, and pass under **St John's Gate**.

Continue down St John's Lane until it merges with St John Street; and then continue onwards to Charterhouse Street. Turn right, and then left down Farringdon Road. Climb the steps onto Holburn Viaduct, and go right. A short distance on the left is the **City Temple**.

Return to Farringdon Road, and continue along it. At Ludgate Circus turn right into Fleet Street. After a short distance on the left is a sign to **St Bride's Church**.

Continue along Fleet Street. On the right is a little alley marked to **Dr Johnson's House**, which is on Gough Square.

At the point where Fleet Street becomes The Strand, turn left down Mitre Court leading to the Temple, in the middle of which stands the **Temple Church**.

ROUTE ONE

St Paul's Cathedral
Cheapside

S Paul's Cathedral and Westminster Abbey compete for the most prestigious religious events. The Queen and Prince Phillip married at Westminster, whereas Charles and Diana chose St Paul's. Most royal funerals are at Westminster, but Winston Churchill was sent on his way at St Paul's.

In fact, St Paul's is the favored venue for war heroes. When Nelson was killed at the Battle of Trafalgar in 1805, his body was pickled in brandy, transported to London, and deposited in the crypt; and a memorial was erected in the south transept — with a lion symbolizing his death in battle. The Duke of Wellington, who survived the Battle of Waterloo in 1815 and went on to become prime minister, is also in the crypt, with a vast memorial in the north aisle showing him on horseback.

St Paul's and Westminster also com-

THE CATHEDRAL WATCHING OVER TRADE AND MONEY-MAKING — A VIEW FROM LONDON BRIDGE.

pete over scientific and artistic geniuses. Westminster wins, but the crypt of St Paul's has, amongst others, William Blake, Arthur Sullivan (H.M.S. Pinafore, etc.),

THE CATHEDRAL LOOKING TOWARDS FLEET STREET — THE 'STREET OF SHAME' WHERE JOURNALISTS ONCE WORKED.

ROUTE ONE

English baroque décor — more restrained than its continental model.

Alexander Fleming (penicillin), and its own architect Christopher Wren. The poet John Donne was dean in the early c17, and from the pulpit he uttered his famous words: 'No man is an island, entire of itself ... any man's death diminishes me, because I am involved in mankind. And therefore never send to know for whom the bell tolls; it tolls for thee.' His effigy is in the south quire aisle; he posed for it during his last illness, wrapping himself in a shroud.

Built by Christopher Wren after the Great Fire of 1666, St Paul's in many people's eyes the finest building in London. But the interior remained rather drab until the nineteenth century when the superb mosaics were installed. In the same period the cathedral acquired William Holman Hunt's *The Light of the World*, showing Christ knocking on a door that opens only on the inside — suggesting that he can only enter our lives if we let him. It is one of the most copied pictures in the world.

After the Second World War the American Memorial Chapel was installed behind the high altar, commemorating the American servicemen who died in Britain. nearby is Henry Moore's exquisite *Mother and Child*, sculpted in 1984.

It is open all day every day 8.30-4; tel 020 7248 3104.

ROUTE ONE

St Mary Le Bow
Cheapside

The great bell hanging in the steeple is called Cuthbert; and if you born within its sound, you can call yourself a Cockney. Christopher Wren, the architect, actually made room for a peal of twelve bells, but Cuthbert didn't receive his full quota of companions until 1907.

The steeple itself is the finest feature of the church – and is also Wren's finest steeple. There are Doric doorways with lolling cherubs; and higher up are Ionic pilaster carrying a fountain of stone. It's a magnificent complement to the dome of St Paul's only a short distance away.

When Wren came to look at the ruins of the medieval church, after the Great Fire of 1666, he found an ancient crypt

A font cover or a wedding cake? Perhaps neither.

with rounded arches; it was from these arches that the name Bow probably comes. Since the arches are made partly from Roman brick, he assumed the entire

Modern craftsmanship in the manner of the original.

ROUTE ONE

construction dated from Roman times. But in fact Norman builders in the CII reused bricks that they must have found nearby. The crypt is now an excellent vegetarian restaurant.

The church was again largely destroyed in the Blitz, although the steeple was miraculously undamaged; and it was rebuilt in the late 1950s according

A COCKNEY IS SOMEONE BORN IN EARSHOT OF THE CHIMES FROM THIS TOWER.

to Wr... with a based ... and th... ...standing against heavy piers are also copied from there. Two pulpits were installed. Originally one was used for leading prayers, and the other for preaching; this was a statement of reconciliation between the Puritans, who exalted preaching, and the High churchmen, who exalted prayer. In recent decades the pulpits have been used for lunchtime dialogues between famous people.

Thomas a Becket, who as archbishop of Canterbury was murdered on the orders of the king, was born near the church in Cheapside. He is remembered in the stained glass window at the west end. The window also includes the arms of the twelve Livery Companies — the ancient London guilds of craftsmen. One of the windows at the east end shows the Virgin Mary cradling the church; the other window shows St Paul surrounded by bombed London churches.

It is open Mon-Thurs 7.30-6, Fri 7.30-4; tel 020 7248 5139.

ROUTE ONE

THE TEMPLE OF MITHRAS
QUEEN VICTORIA STREET

In 1954, when an office block was being built, the foundations of a Roman temple were found. Archeologists lifted the foundations stone by stone, and re-laid them nearby on their present site. It was a long, narrow building, and at one end there is the outline of a semi-circular apse where an altar would have stood — so it conforms to the usual design of a temple to the deity Mithras.

Devotion to Mithras was remarkably widespread. He was, and still is, worshipped in Hinduism as Mitra. He played a vital role in the ancient Iranian religion associated with the prophet Zoroaster, keeping the peace between the spirit of goodness and the spirit of evil. The wise men, who came from the east to worship the infant Jesus in Bethlehem, were probably Zoroastrian priests, known as 'magi'.

Then between the second and fifth centuries CE Mithras became popular amongst the Romans. Soldiers and government officials seem to have been especially keen; and temples were most commonly built in the border regions, such as along the Rhine and the Danube. This suggests that Mithras was regarded as an upholder of the established order, and an enemy of barbarism. Thus by placing a temple to Mithras in the center of the capital city, the Roman imperialists were asserting their intention to civilize the barbarian Britons. When the Roman legions departed in 400, the Britons quickly reverted to their old barbarian ways — suggesting that Mithras doesn't share Roman social prejudices.

ROUTE ONE

His Roman devotees regarded Mithras as the father and creator of the universe; and the temple was built and decorated to look like a cave, which represented the

ROMAN CITIZENS MAY ONCE HAVE CELEBRATED CHRISTMAS HERE — BUT BEFORE CHRISTIANITY CAME TO BRITAIN.

universe. The temple probably contained some kind of sculpture or relief that showed Mithras slaying a bull, symbolizing his victory over evil. There may also have been a relief depicting the birth of Mithras; he emerged from a rock as a young adult, accompanied by two torch-bearers.

The birth of Mithras may have been celebrated on December 25 — his festival later taken over by Christians to celebrate the birth of Christ.

It can be seen at any time, and is floodlit at night.

AN ALTAR WHERE BULLS MAY ONCE HAVE BEEN SACRIFICED TO AN IRANIAN GOD.

ROUTE ONE

St Magnus the Martyr
Lower Thames Street

Just outside the entrance of the church, in the archway under the tower, is a fossilized hulk of timber that was part of the Roman quayside, built nearby in c1. And in the entrance hall of the church is a model of the old London Bridge, demolished in late c18, with shops and houses built along it, and a chapel in the middle. These are reminders that from Roman times until quite recently St Magnus Church stood at London's entrance, with the nation's imports and exports passing by. Indeed, the archway was created in 1756 to widen the access to the quay. The entrance also has shelves where bread was left for the poor — a reminder that amidst London's wealth there was destitution.

For many centuries this was the church that the Lord Mayor of London attended each Sunday. He was accompanied by a sword-bearer, who placed the weapon on a sword-rest. This splendid piece of metalwork, which is near the front of the church on the north side, has little shields displaying the arms of three mayors and two livery companies.

Opposite is one of the finest pulpits in London, dating from c17. The wrought iron communion rails date from the same period. The huge organ at the west end was built in 1712, and was the first instrument to have a 'swell' — a shutter that the organist can slide in front of the pipe box to regulate the volume.

Miles Coverdale is buried in the south-east corner. He translated the whole Bible

THE BASE OF THIS TOWER IS THE OLD GATEWAY TO LONDON.

into English, and this was the first translation to be printed. His version of the psalms is used in the Anglican *Book of Common Prayer*.

St Magnus himself stands on the south wall. He was a joint ruler of Orkney in the early C12, and allowed himself to be murdered in order to avoid a civil war with his fellow ruler. The statue was installed in the middle of C20. Since he was of Viking descent, he has a horned helmet on his head, and a fine battle-axe in his right hand; he holds a model of the church in his left hand.

Sadly in 1921 an office block was erect-

ONE OF LONDON'S FINEST PULPITS.

ed on the south side, cutting off the church from the river. The road on the north side is a noisy dual carriageway, and to the east is another dreary modern building. The church is thus an oasis of calm beauty amidst the worst of the modern city.

It is open Tues-Fri 10-4, Sun 9.30-1; tel 020 7626 4481.

MOSES AND AARON IN ENGLISH GARB STAND ON EITHER SIDE OF THE ALTAR.

ROUTE ONE

SOUTHWARK CATHEDRAL

Shakespeare's Globe Theatre, recently re-erected under the inspiration of Sam Wanamaker, stands nearby. Shakespeare is commemorated with a sculpture and a window on the south side of the nave. The sculpture, carved in 1912, shows him reclining, set against a background of seventeenth-century Southwark. The window above, erected in 1954, has figures from his plays, including a hairy Caliban from *The Tempest*, Hamlet with Yorick's skull, and the defeated Richard III dreaming of exchanging his kingdom for a horse.

Further up the cathedral near the high altar is the splendid tomb of Lancelot Andrewes, showing him in somber episcopal robes, with a book in his hand. He was the major compiler of *The King James Bible*,

THE CATHEDRAL WAS REBUILT AFTER A FIRE IN 1212, WHICH DESTROYED MOST OF SOUTHWARK.

and also composed eloquent prayers and sermons. His sermon about the wise men includes the wonderfully evocative words: 'A cold coming they had of it, at this time of the year: just the worst time of the year to take a journey, and especially a long journey. The way is deep, the weather sharp, the day is short, the very dead of winter.' — words that T.S.Eliot lifted for his famous

LIONEL LOCKYER, WHO MADE A FORTUNE SELLING PILLS FOR EVERY DISEASE, IS RESTING.

poem *Journey of the Magi*, with phrases that have passed into common usage.

As bishop of Winchester in Shakespeare's time Andrewes diocese stretched from the English Channel to the Thames; and his palace was nearby — so this was his main church. Southwark only became a separate diocese covering south London, and this church its cathedral, in 1905.

On the opposite side is a chapel commemorating John Harvard, founder of Harvard University, who was baptized in this church in 1607. The window above the altar

THIS IS THE FOURTH ROOF; THE FIRST BURNT AND THE SECOND COLLAPSED.

THE SHAKESPEARE WINDOW — SPOT THE REFERENCES TO HIS PLAYS.

shows the coat of arms of Emmanuel College, Cambridge, where Harvard himself was educated.

Nearby in the north transept, is the comical monument of a quack doctor, Lionel Lockyer. Despite his pills, which are eulogized in a poem, he died at quite an early age in 1673.

In 1520 an earlier bishop of Winchester installed the huge stone screen behind the high altar; but it had to wait until 1905 for the figures to be added. Beyond the high altar are four small chapels, one of which is dedicated to the victims of AIDS.

To the north of the cathedral a visitors' center was built in 1988, showing the history of the cathedral and the area. And to mark the millennium a refectory was added.

It is open daily 8-6; tel 020 7407 3708.

ROUTE ONE

Spanish and Portuguese Synagogue
Bevis Marks

The Jews in Europe have long been famous for their financial acumen; and while Christians have been willing to borrow from Jews, they have also resented the Jews for their wealth. However, the Jews turned to financial activity as a consequence of Christian persecution: in much of medieval Europe Jews were prohibited from owning land, so banking and money lending were their only means of survival.

Until the Nazis plumbed new depths of anti-Semitic horror, the worst persecution occurred in Spain, when the Inquisition drove the Jews out of the country. Many settled in Holland; and while the Spanish economy gradually declined, Dutch prosperity, aided by the Jewish immigrants, rose rapidly. Oliver Cromwell, anxious about the English economy, actively encouraged Jewish immigration — and from the 1650s onwards the Jewish community in the city of London steadily grew.

The first Jews from Holland worshipped in an upstairs room in Creechurch Lane, where they sat on simple benches without backs. In 1701 a sympathetic Quaker, in act of remarkable financial and spiritual generosity, built them a synagogue. Benches with backs were installed; but for nostalgia' sake the backless benches were placed in the northwest corner.

The shape on the synagogue is that of a church, and the style is classical; the Jews wanted to seem as normal as possible to English eyes. The ark at the east end, where huge scrolls of the *Torah* are kept, is like a church reredos. The main difference is that the Ten Commandments are inscribed in Hebrew, not English — the negative ones on the left, and the positive ones on the right. During the main service on Saturday mornings one of the scrolls is

16

ROUTE ONE

resigned his membership, and he and his family were baptized as Anglicans.

It is open every day except Thurs and Sat 11.30-1.00; tel 020 7626 1274.

EACH CANDELABRUM REPRESENTS ONE OF THE DAYS IT TOOK GOD TO MAKE THE WORLD.

carried to a large lectern at the west end, and unrolled at the passage for the week.

Seven huge brass candelabra, each with a large ball at the center, hang from the ceiling; and genuine candles still burn from them. The biggest candelabrum in the middle represents the world; the other six represent the days it took for God to create the world.

Twelve pillars painted like marble, representing the twelve tribes of Israel, hold up a gallery where women sit. At the back of the gallery are boards with the names of the leading members of the synagogue. These include Isaac Disraeli, father of Benjamin who became Prime Minister under Queen Victoria. After an argument over money Isaac Disraeli

ROUTE ONE

East London Central Mosque
Whitechapel Road

The east end of London has long been the gateway for poor immigrants: they remain here for one or two generations; and as they become more prosperous, they move to more salubrious areas. Irish arrived in the mid c19 fleeing the famine, and then came Jews from eastern Europe fleeing pogroms. The most recent wave of immigration is from Bangladesh; impoverished Bangladeshis began to arrive in the 1950s, encouraged by the British government in order to meet an acute labor shortage.

Most of the Bangladeshis are Sunni Muslims. Originally they worshipped in converted houses and shops; and this remains the pattern in most part of Britain. But in 1982 the Bangladeshis of east London decided to build a proper mosque. They chose as their main materials yellow and red bricks, echoing the polychrome brickwork often used in Arab lands; and they erected some quite modest minarets – fearful that anything more conspicuous might cause antagonism. The result, while of no particular architectural merit, fits happily into its surroundings.

There are separate entrances for men and women. The men's entrance leads to the main body of the mosque. The women's entrance leads up to a gallery overlooking the mosque; and they peer through thick net curtains to the proceedings below.

The floor of the mosque is covered with a green carpet, which has a pattern

ROUTE ONE

THE MIHRAB, FROM WHERE SERMONS ARE PREACHED, FACES MECCA.

The windows are shaped in a simplified version of the traditional Islamic style. And around the walls are a series of blank Islamic arches that contain huge electric storage heaters — so even on a cold day the mosque is warm.

Two stairways, one from the entrance hall and the other from the mosque itself, lead down to a large chamber for ablutions, with rows of taps. In the entrance hall there is a small shop stuffed with books in Bengali and English on Islam, with some charming illustrated books for children. But sadly no one has written a history and guide of the mosque itself.

It is open daily 10-10; tel 020 7247 1357.

FROM THIS MINARET THE MUSLIMS OF EAST LONDON ARE CALLED TO PRAYER.

of Islamic arches; each arch defines the space in which a man sits and kneels during Friday prayers. Above is a dome, which is plain apart from texts from the Quran inscribed around the base. The walls too are plain, apart from a green frieze half way up.

ROUTE ONE

JAMME MASJID MOSQUE
BRICK LANE

The Protestant Reformation began quite separately in Germany and France; Germany produced Martin Luther as the major leader, and France produced John Calvin. And from the start the French Protestants faced far fiercer persecution that their German counterparts. Calvin was forced into exile in 1534, and thereafter devoted most of his efforts to creating a religious utopia in Geneva. But his ideas flowed back into France, and guided the development of the Huguenot church — as the reformed church in France

THIS OLD CHURCH DOESN'T FACE MECCA, BUT ITS NEW MIHRAB (ALCOVE) DOES.

became known.

A long series of wars between the Huguenots and the French monarchy concluded with a treaty known as the Edict of Nantes. But when this was revoked in 1685, almost half a million Huguenots fled the country — and many arrived in London. The majority, like later waves of immigrants, settled in the east end. Soon they began to prosper, and in 1743 they built themselves a magnificent church.

Eventually the Huguenots integrated fully into English society, and no longer wanted to worship separately. So the Bangladeshi Muslims purchased the church, and converted it into a mosque. Brick Lane, in which it stands, has become the main shopping street for the Bangladeshi community, where you can buy delicious Indian sweetmeats and silk saris. Even the street signs are in Bengali as well as English.

There are two sets of windows: the lower set are relatively small, with flattened arches; while the upper set are tall, with rounded arches. Originally the upper set would have bathed the church in natural light. But the Muslims have installed a gallery, held up by classical columns, covering most of the space. The women sit there, listening to the iman through an octagonal hole, while the men are shrouded in gloom.

Happily the brass candelabra have been preserved, the biggest of which pokes through the hole. But modern lights have been put on the walls. The walls themselves are mostly plain plaster, apart from some old paneling on one side; everything has been painted cream.

A mihrah (niche) for the iman has been made in one corner, surrounded in white and fawn marble. As in many English mosques, the carpet pattern is a series of Islamic arches, each defining a space for a man to sit and kneel; it has been laid diagonally, so the men face the imam.

It is open daily 10-4; tel 020 7247 6052.

THE CHURCH BUILT BY FRENCH HUGUENOTS IN THE HEART OF BANGLADESHI LONDON.

ROUTE ONE

John Wesley's House and Museum
City Road

John Wesley, the founder of Methodism, grew up in a strictly religious house. And as a student at Oxford, training for the Anglican ministry, he initiated a society known as the Holy Club, dedicated to instilling greater 'method' in its members' religious observance; this included regular prayers, and a program of charitable works. But his method provided no inward peace, and he was wracked by guilt; and although he was now ordained, he came to regard his religion as a sham.

Then in 1738, at the age of 35, he had a spiritual experience transforming his faith: his heart was 'strangely warmed', which he interpreted as Christ entering it. He spent the rest of his life urging others to let Christ into their hearts. To this end he toured Britain and America on horseback, traveling a quarter of a million miles, and preaching forty thousand sermons, mostly in the open air outside factory gates or on village greens. And wherever he won converts, he formed a Methodist society to nurture them. His brother Charles composed hymns, set to popular tunes of the day, for the converts to sing. And, along with George Whitefield, the Wesley brothers were the pioneers of the Evangelical revival — which remains remarkably vigorous.

A PULPIT FOR JOHN WESLEY'S RARE INDOOR SERMONS — HE PREFERRED OPEN FIELDS.

The first Methodist society was in London. In 1739 he took over a disused cannon foundry, and within a few years over a thousand people were meeting there each week. For forty years it also served as the headquarters for the entire Methodist movement. Wesley hoped that Methodism would remain within the Anglican fold, acting as a spiritual stimulus. But most Anglican clergy hated it, while ardent Methodists despised Anglicanism for its laxity. So by the 1770s

AN ORNATE CHURCH FOR A MAN OF AUSTERE SIMPLICITY.

Methodism had virtually become a separate church; and John Wesley obtained this site on which to build his own chapel.

Although Wesley's ministry was mainly to the poor, Methodism had now become fashionable. King George III donated redundant ship's masts to support the gallery. And the rich and famous were eager to attend the opening service – the ladies' elaborate hats so upset Wesley that he devoted the first fifteen minutes of his sermon to denouncing them. Wesley's pulpit survives. Wesley lived next to the chapel, sharing his house with other preachers. He died here on March 2, 1791 – and the preaching plan displayed inside the house shows the he continued preaching to within a few days of his death.

The Methodist Church claims a worldwide membership of 70 million, making it larger than the Anglican Communion – although in England it has declined more rapidly.

A museum of Methodism adjoins the chapel. The chapel, house and museum are open Mon-Sat 10-4, and Sun 12-2 Sun; tel 020 7253 2262.

ROUTE ONE

St John's Church and Gate
St John's Square

After the success of the first crusade in capturing Jerusalem in 1099, the pope sanctioned the formation of the Knights Hospitaller, whose primary aim was to provide hospitality for Christian pilgrims, and care for those that fell sick. It also established an army to defend the pilgrims. Although the knights took the monastic vows of poverty, obedience and chastity, they became increasingly militaristic, and also accumulated vast wealth.

St John's Gate was built in 1504 to provide a grand entrance to their London branch. The gate was entered from the south, and led into a complex of monastic buildings, at the center of which was the great Church of St John. However, soon afterwards King Henry VIII suppressed the order in England, and in 1540 he seized its London buildings. Many were destroyed, but the gate and the church remained. In the early c18 the gate was a coffee house, and in c19 it was the Old Jerusalem Tavern.

In the fashionable spirit of medieval revivalism, the order was revived in England in the c19, receiving a royal char-

A GATE FOR WEALTHY CHRISTIAN KNIGHTS BACK FROM THE ORIENT.

ter from Queen Victoria; and the gate, after much restoration became its new headquarters. Although its members luxuriated in colorful uniforms and ceremonies, they now had no military pretensions. Their main work was — and is — running the St John Ambulance Brigade, which provides a voluntary first aid service at public events.

On the ground floor there is a delightful museum showing the ancient and recent history of the order; and the rooms themselves, paneled in neo-Tudor style, are charming. Above the gate is the Council Chamber, where monthly meetings are held. The roof has its original c16 trusses, and the fireplace dates from 1700.

Next to the Council Chamber is the Chancery, which has a remarkable collection of silver; the Knights used to serve their patients from silver as a symbol of respect. This in turn leads into the Chapter Hall built in 1902. The main interest is the corbels, each of which displays the shield of one of the Tongues of the original order; the order was organized according to language, and each division was called a Tongue. There is a c17 cabinet with at least 50 hidden drawers.

St John's Church was bombed in the Second World War, and has been reconstructed. Next to it is a memorial garden surrounded by cloisters – a mixture of old and new. Beneath it is the original crypt, some of which dates from c12. It contains a monument from late c15 of a Castilian knight, and the tomb of the last medieval prior – showing him as an emaciated corpse.

The museum is open Mon-Fri 10-5, and Sat 10-4. Guided tours of the whole Gate, Church and Crypt are on Tues, Fri and Sat at 11 and 2.30. Tel 020 7253 6644.

A MEMORIAL GARDEN WHERE A GERMAN BOMB DESTROYED THE CHURCH.

ROUTE ONE

CITY TEMPLE
HOLBURN VIADUCT

The Catholic and Anglican churches have emphasized their various offices, such as archbishop, bishop, and priest; and the individual occupying a particular office at a particular time is less important than the office itself. Evangelical groups by contrast are more concerned with the spiritual gifts that an individual may pos-

A PLACE FOR SAVING THE SOULS IN THE HEART OF DICKENS' LONDON.

sess, and especially the gift of preaching. Thus throughout c19 charismatic preachers attracted vast congregations; and to house these congregations great halls were built — variously known as temple and tabernacles, as well as churches and chapels.

One of these great Victorian preachers was Joseph Parker; and the City Temple was erected for the thousands that flocked to hear him each Sunday.

Parker was born in northern England

in 1830, and came to London in 1869 to take over a small, independent congregation that was originally led by Thomas Goodwin, chaplain to Oliver Cromwell. It met in various private homes, and was Congregationalist — the people ran in on democratic lines. But as word of Parker's oratory spread, the congregation exploded, and soon no home or existing chapel was big enough. So in 1874 a huge sum was raised to construct a neo-classical edifice in golden sandstone. The Holburn Viaduct had just been completed, and it was the first building to open directly onto it — although it has a lower story beneath the Viaduct.

Just before preaching Parker washed his long, curly hair, so that it appeared wet and shiny. And gradually, as his sermon progressed, his hair dried and became fluffy. Thus unlike most preachers, who sweated with tension as they declaimed, he gave the impression of becoming calmer and more relaxed. Parker considered standing for parliament, on a program that included the prohibition of alcohol and the abolition of the special privileges of the Church of England. But he withdrew when it became clear he would lose.

The trouble with the Evangelical approach is that, when the preacher dies, his congregation goes into a slow decline; and this has been the experience of the City Temple since Parker's death in 1902. The church was bombed in the Second World War, although happily the grand front was left standing. Perhaps foolishly, the Rockefeller family in America was persuaded to donate a substantial sum for the rebuilding; and the present church, attached to the original front, was opened in 1958. It is mainly modern in style; but it has a pulpit that looks strangely like a box in the theater, and its walls have a blue and white frieze in the style of Wedgwood pottery.

It is open on request; tel 020 7583 5532.

AN OASIS OF SILENCE FOR PEOPLE OF ALL RACES.

ROUTE ONE

ST BRIDE'S CHURCH
FLEET STREET

THE CHURCH WHERE JOURNALISTS PRAY, AND ARE PRAYED FOR.

The tiered steeple of St Bride's — Christopher Wren's highest — is said to have inspired the first tiered wedding cake. Each of the four tiers is identical, except that the columns grow shorter and the arches narrower, while the pedestals grow higher; so the steeple seems to thrust upwards into the sky like a rocket. Happily the steeple escaped the bombardment that gutted the church in 1940.

After the War the site was excavated, and a Roman pavement and burial site were discovered; so this has been sacred ground for almost two millennia. The church was then rebuilt according to Wren's design. The old pews, however, were replaced by collegiate style seating that encloses almost the entire nave, giving the church a rather intimate atmosphere. There are modern statues of St Bride and St Paul at the west end.

A huge rerodos was also installed after the War, with a painting of the crucifixion by Glyn Jones. He also painted the east wall behind the reredos. He was inspired

THE INSPIRATION FOR THE TIERED WEDDING CAKE.

A BRIGHT MODERN CRUCIFIXION; BEHIND IS A CELESTIAL CHOIR.

by a description, written in 1708, of an earlier painting: 'above the clouds appears (from within a large crimson festoon painted curtain) a celestial choir or representation of the church triumphant.'

The first printing press in London was sited here in 1500; and Wynkyn de Worde, the first man to print music in England, was buried here in 1534. And in c19 Fleet Street became the home of almost all the national newspapers. So St Bride's became the church of journalists and printers. And when the journalist John Macarthy was held hostage in Beirut, a vigil was kept for him here.

Sadly in the 1980s St Brides lost its spiritual parish. The printers, fearing loss of jobs and earnings, bitterly resisted the introduction of computerized typesetting; and this led to a series of bitter confrontations with the newspaper proprietors. Eventually the proprietors decided to abandon Fleet Street, and start afresh elsewhere; so the newspapers are now dispersed.

St Bride's has some further claims to distinction. The marriage took place here in 1575 of the parents of the first white child to be born in colonial America. A few years later Thomas Weelkes, the great composer of madrigals, was buried here. And in 1633 Samuel Pepys was baptized here; his famous diaries provide our main record of the Great Fire.

It is open every day 8-5; tel 020 7353 1301.

ROUTE ONE

Dr Johnson's House
17 Gough Square, off Fleet Street

Samuel Johnson is most famous for his dictionary, which was commissioned by a group of booksellers in 1747, and first appeared eight years later. His definitions were both accurate and quirky. He defined oats as 'a grain, which in England is generally given to horses, but in Scotland supports the people'; and he defined his own profession of lexicographer as 'a harmless drudge'. He employed several scribes to assist him in this drudgery; and he rented the house in Gough Square to provide enough space, staying there until 1759. However his great work was not the first work of its kind; and, although it defined 40,000 words, nor was it the fullest. A dictionary by Nathaniel Bailey both preceded and exceeded Johnson's. But Johnson's work was the first to contain quotations showing the various shades of meaning of each word.

The main work on the dictionary took place in the garret, which now has copies of the pieces of paper on which Johnson

A HARMLESS DRUDGE AND A LITERARY MAN OF PRAYER.

wrote definitions and quotations. The rest of the house is filled with portraits of people who played a part in Johnson's life. These include his beloved wife, Elizabeth, a wealthy widow who was twenty years his senior; her portrait is in the Will Room. As the name implies, his will is displayed there; he left most of his estate to his black servant Francis Barber, whose portrait hangs in the parlor.

Johnson's wit and verbal dexterity also served him well as a journalist and raconteur. But beneath his worldly exterior was a man of deep religious devotion, who wrote at length about the moral and spiritual issues of his time, and composed elegant and moving prayers. Indeed, one of his prayers related to the compiling of the dictionary: 'O God, who hast hitherto supported me, enable me to proceed in this labor, and in the whole task of my present state; that when I shall render up at the last day an account of the talent committed to me, I may receive pardon.' And after the death of his wife he wrote a series of prayers in which he described his grief and begged God for comfort.

His religiosity stemmed from his parents. His father, a somewhat impecunious bookseller in the town of Lichfield, was high church in his sympathies. His mother was a stern puritan, and required him to learn by heart the Anglican collects, plus large portions of the Bible in the Authorized version -a wonderful training for a writer.

THE FAVORITE COMPANION WHO NOW CAN NEVER STRAY.

A sculpture of Dr Johnson's cat Hodge stands outside in the square. A statue of Dr Johnson himself stands nearby in the Strand, at the east side of St Clement Danes Church.

The house is open Mon-Sat 11-5 Mon-Sat; tel 020 7353 3745.

THE HOUSE WHERE THE DICTIONARY WAS COMPILED.

ROUTE ONE

Temple Church

Shortly after the Knights Hosptallers had formed to protect pilgrims to Jerusalem, an even more militaristic order formed with a similar function, the Knights Templars. In 1118 the initial group took a solemn vow to patrol the pilgrim routes and destroy any bandits. The order rapidly grew, and soon they were building castles throughout the eastern Mediterranean. They also acquired large amounts of gold and silver, which they deposited in 'temples' in London and Paris; and thus they became the major bankers of medieval Europe. They were

ONE OF THE MASTERS, MINISTERING TO LAWYERS' SOULS.

vowed to celibacy, and wore a white habit with a red cross; and they recruited large numbers of ordinary soldiers to support them.

The west end of the Temple Church, built in 1185, was their London temple, stacked with precious metal; it is circular in imitation of the Holy Sepulcher Church in Jerusalem. The long rectangular choir was added in 1240 as a place of worship. Presumably — although there is evidence of this — there was a partition between the two, separating God from Mammon

THE ORIGINAL ENTRANCE TO A CRUSADER TEMPLE.

ROUTE ONE

The Templars wealth inspired envy amongst the kings and nobles of Europe, the pope disbanded them in 1338. In the rest of England various powerful barons seized their estates, while the king took possession of the church in London and its surrounding buildings. The king then rented the buildings to two groups of lawyers, who came to be identified as the Inner and Middle Temples; and they shared the church. After the Reformation the lawyers appointed the priest, known as the Master, and the organist — although for over a century they disagreed so violently on styles of music that they each appointed their own organist, who played on alternate Sundays.

The church was greatly restored in 1840-2, and was badly bombed in 1941. But the west entrance is unchanged. And the vaulted ceiling of the choir miraculously survived the bombing, as the heat spread through the porous limestone quickly and evenly. But the marble columns supporting it cracked, and had to be replaced.

The effigies of the crusaders at the west end were smashed into pieces by the bomb, but have been lovingly restored. Nearby is the splendid tomb of a lawyer, Edmund Plowden, who died in 1584; he is described as being a man of 'great gravity,

LONDON'S ANSWER TO JERUSALEM'S HOLY SEPULCHER.

knowledge and integrity.

Outside the church, on the north side, is the elegant reclining figure of John Hiccocks, a Master who died in 1726. Nearby is the tomb of the playwright Oliver Goldsmith. In the courtyard to the south there is a millennium statue of Knights Templar on horseback.

It is open most days, but at irregular times; tel 020 7353 3470.

ROUTE TWO

WEST LONDON

👉 Start at **Westminster Abbey**.

Coming out of the Abbey turn left along Victoria Street. Turn right into Buckingham Gate. On the left is **Westminster Chapel**.

Turn left beside the chapel, down Castle Lane, and left at the end into Palace Street. This leads back to Victoria Street. Diagonally opposite, set back from the street, is **Westminster Cathedral**.

Continue along Victoria Street to Victoria station. Take the tube two stops to South Kensington station (District and Circle lines westbound). Come out of the station exit marked to the Natural History Museum, and turn left up Cromwell Gardens. On the left is the **Brompton Oratory**.

Behind the Brompton Oratory at the end of Cottage Place is **Holy Trinity Church**.

Return to South Kensington station, and take the tube one stop to Sloane Square (District and Circle lines eastbound). Coming out of the station turn left, and then left again down Lower Sloane Street, which become Chelsea Bridge Road. Cross Chelsea Bridge, and on the other side go right along the river path. This leads to the **Peace Pagoda**.

Continue along the river, cross Albert Bridge, and turn left into Cheyne Walk. On the right is **Chelsea Old Church**.

Continue along Cheyne Walk, which becomes Cremorne Road. This makes a half turn to the right, becoming Ashburn Road, which becomes Gunter Grove, which becomes Finborough Road. Turn left along Old Brompton Road, and a short distance on the left is West Brompton station. Take the tube seven stops to Wimbledon (District line southbound). Coming out of the station turn right along Wimbledon Hill Road, which becomes Wimbledon High Street, and then Parkside. Turn right into Calonne Road. At No. 14 is the **Buddhapadipa Temple**.

Return to Wimbledon station and take the tube eight stops to Earl's Court (District line northbound). Then take eight stops to Covent Garden (Piccadilly line eastbound). Coming out of the station turn left down James Street, which leads into Covent Garden.

ROUTE TWO

On the right side of Covent Garden is **St Paul's Church**.

Go out of Covent Garden on the opposite side. Turn left into Bow Street, which becomes Endell Street. At the top turn left into St Giles High Street, which leads to Tottenham Court Road station. Take the tube four stops (Central line westbound) to Lancaster Gate station. Coming out of the station turn left along Bayswater Road. At Victoria Gate of the **Pet Cemetery**.

Take the train back to Tottenham Court Road station. Coming out of the station turn right along Oxford Street, and then turn left to Soho Square. On the right, just before entering the square, is the **Radha Krishna Temple**.

Return to Oxford Street, turn right, and continue past Oxford Circus to Bond Street station. Go none stops to Neasden (Jubilee line northbound). Coming out of the station

turn right along Neaden Lane. At a roundabout turn right along Church Road; and as this bears left, turn right into Craven Park. Then turn right along Brentfield Road. Some distance along, on the left, is the **Swaminarayan Hindu Temple**. The walk from the station takes about 30 minutes; alternatively, there is a No. 16 bus to Tescos, and then a No. 206 bus.

Return to Neasden station, and go seven stops to St John's Wood (Jubilee line southbound). Coming out of the station turn left down Wellington Road, and at the roundabout go straight across into Park Road. On the left is the **London Central Mosque**.

Return to Green Park station, and go back along Piccadilly. Shortly before Piccadilly Circus **St James's Church** is on the right.

ROUTE TWO

WESTMINSTER ABBEY

This is the church of England's kings and queens: they have been crowned here, and many are buried here. Queens Mary and Elizabeth — Bloody Mary and Good Queen Bess — share a tomb, despite their rivalry and religious differences. Henry VII, their grandfather, built a chapel with a vaulted ceiling of breath-taking intricacy, to be a burial place for Henry VI; but he himself found his final resting-place here in a tomb of great splendor, which he shares with his wife.

Four centuries earlier Edward the Confessor built the first great church on this site for his own burial; and his death in 1066 triggered the rapid series of events that led to the Norman conquest. In 1102 Edward's body was inspected, and — so the inspectors reported — the flesh was entirely intact. This was a sign of sanctity, and a campaign began for his canonization. The pope was initially resistant; but miracles began to occur at Edward's tomb, and eventually in 1163 he was officially declared a saint. Henry III rebuilt the choir and the sanctuary, and Italian craftsmen were employed to create a shrine. The shrine was defaced at the

THE CLOISTER WHERE MONKS ONCE COPIED SACRED TEXTS.

Protestant Reformation, but Queen Mary, a devout Catholic, had it restored.

Westminster Abbey is also the church where literature — the art in which England excels — is celebrated, with statues and memorials to her finest poets and novelists. The first great poet of the English language, Geoffrey Chaucer, was buried in the south transept, not for his literary efforts, but because he was clerk of works. A century and a half after his death, when his literary prowess had been recognized, his tomb was much embellished; and this tomb acted as a magnet for other literary burials and memorials. Edmund Spenser and Charles Dickens are interred here, as are the historian Lord Macaulay and the actors David Garrick and Henry Irving. Shakespeare had to wait over a century for a monument, but more recent giants of letters, such as Henry James, T.S. Eliot and W.H. Auden, have been acknowledged more quickly.

It is both a blessing and a curse for churches with a high profile that successive generations want to make their mark. The Abbey has architectural features of varying quality from every century. But few would quibble with the twin towers ate the west end. Built in 1745 by the architect Nicholas Hawksmoor, following original designs by Christopher Wren, they are a magnificent mix of gothic and classical features.

The Abbey is open every day 8-6; tel 020 7222 5152.

THE WEST TOWERS, DESIGNED BY CHRISTOPHER WREN AND MODIFIED BY NICHOLAS HAWKSMOOR IN 1745.

ROUTE TWO

Westminster Chapel
Buckingham Gate

History is highly selective: most people famous during their lifetimes are entirely forgotten after they die; while people who labored in obscurity enjoyed posthumous celebration. In the late c19 one of the three or four most renowned religious figures in Britain — alongside such luminaries as William Booth, C.H. Spurgeon and Cardinal Newman — was a minister called Samuel Martin. But the homely imagery and innocent humor of his sermons is so dated as to be barely comprehensible today; and his philanthropic works have long been superceded. So he is almost entirely forgotten. Only his splendid church remains, a beacon amidst the anonymity of expensive offices and apartments that now crowd this area to the south of Buckingham Palace.

A century and a half ago, despite the proximity of royalty, it was one of the poorest areas in London; and in its midst stood an old hospital struggling to deal with rampant disease. The hospital itself became so foul that it was forced to close; and in 1841 Samuel Martin, then a young man, was invited to found a chapel on the site. His original chapel was completed in 1843; and he then built a school for poor children just behind it. The school building, in simple classical style, remains, now serving as a meeting hall; it can be seen clearly from Castle Lane. In 1859 Martin added a series of alms-houses for the poor to the left of the chapel; these also remain, and were later extended.

By 1864 his fame was so great and his services so popular that he decided to

A MONUMENT TO ONE OF THE GREAT VICTORIAN PREACHERS.

build a much larger chapel; and this still stands, virtually unaltered both outside and in. The exterior is in the style of a traditional Italian church, although built of yellow London brick. The interior forms a huge auditorium, with raked seating at ground level, and two galleries above, each extending almost all the way round the building. At the end of each pew is a device for holding walking sticks and umbrellas. Vast radiators, consisting of several Grecian columns painted gold, warm the congregation.

The focus of the chapel is a huge circular pulpit, which has space not just for the

THE HUGE PULPIT, WITH SPACE FOR THE PREACHER TO LEAP ABOUT

RADIATORS TO LOOK LIKE THE FRONT OF A GREEK TEMPLE.

preacher, but for several people sitting behind him. Beneath the pulpit is a great wooden throne on which the minister leading the service sits; it was made in Italy, and its arms rest on two winged lions, intricately carved, that represent St Mark the evangelist. Rising behind the pulpit is a grand organ — Martin knew that a solid sermon had to be leavened by hearty singing.

The chapel is open on request; tel 020 7834 1731.

ROUTE TWO

WESTMINSTER CATHEDRAL
VICTORIA STREET

Cardinal Manning, the founder of Westminster Cathedral, initially wanted a parliamentary career; but his father's bankruptcy forced him to find employment with a regular salary, so he became a civil servant. He then decided to seek ordination in the Church of England, and became a curate in Sussex, marrying the rector's daughter. At this stage he was evangelical, and regarded the pope as the enemy of true faith; he even preached a sermon on the subject at Oxford university. However, he came to regard the Church of England as lax on matters of doctrine; and after visiting Rome and meeting the pope, he concluded that the Catholic church was the only reliable repository of divine truth.

In 1851 he was ordained a Catholic priest. He rapidly climbed the hierarchy, and in 1865 he was made archbishop of Westminster — the head of the Catholic church in England. He devoted most of his enormous energy to building schools for Catholic children — who were mainly the offspring of Irish immigrants — and shelters for the homeless. But as his crowning achievement he wanted to build a Catholic cathedral in Westminster to rival the Abbey.

Happily a dilapidated prison a short distance to the west the Abbey was closed; and, as the prisoners moved out, Manning acquired the funds to buy the site. By now the fashion for gothic architecture was waning, and the favored style for ecclesiastical buildings was 'byzantine' — inspired by churches of the ancient Byzantine empire. So John Francis

ROUTE TWO

Bentley, a leading exponent of the style, was hired as architect; and the Santa Sophia of Istanbul was recreated within earshot of Victoria station, amidst slums and brothels. Sadly, Manning never lived

to see it; he died in 1892, and the foundation stone was not laid until three years later. But when it was completed his body was moved here from Kensal Green Cemetery.

The materials used in decorating the church were purchased from far afield — honey-colored marble from Verona, green marble from Thessaly, oak and walnut from Austria, and ivory from India. But the jewels of the cathedral are the mosaics, and these continue to be commissioned — most recently the mosaic of St Patrick, dedicated in 1999. The artist and typographer Eric Gill, famous for designing the London Underground logo, was responsible for the stations of the cross on the nave columns. When it was later revealed that he was a pedophile with incestuous inclinations, some people thought his work should be banished; but artistic sensitivities prevailed. He also did the sculpture above the altar in St George's chapel.

The cathedral is open 7-7; tel 020 7798 9055.

A BYZANTINE EXTRAVAGANZA FOR ROMAN CATHOLICS IN PROTESTANT ENGLAND.

ROUTE TWO

BROMPTON ORATORY
BROMPTON ROAD

ONE OF MANY ALTARS — EVERY PRIEST HAS HIS OWN.

When the young Yorkshireman, Frederick Faber, arrived at Oxford, he came under the influence of John Henry Newman, thirteen years his senior. Newman was a leading figure in the Tractarian movement, publishing tracts that urged Anglicanism to rediscover its doctrinal and liturgical roots in the pre-Reformation church. And when in 1842 Faber became priest of a country parish near Peterborough, he tried to expound these ideas, and introduce ancient rituals. His parishioners were resistant.

In October 1845 Newman, now convinced that the Church of England was hopelessly mired in heresy, joined the Roman Catholic Church; and six weeks later Faber followed him. They were both duly ordained as Catholic priests, and in 1848 they formed an oratory in Birmingham, based on the oratory formed by Philip Neri in Florence in c16 — a community of priests engaged in pastoral activities. But Newman became irritated by Faber's flamboyant style, while Faber felt constrained by Newman's somber pessimism. So they split, with Newman remaining in Birmingham, while Faber found a site in Brompton, then a suburb of London — 'a neighborhood of second-rate gentry and second-rate shops', as Newman snootily described it.

Faber devoted himself both to caring for the local poor, and to writing numerous hymns and devotional books. Others joined him, and money flowed in; by 1854 a house for the priests and a rather plain church were complete. But, exhausted by his efforts, Faber died in 1863, aged only 49.

In 1874 the Duke of Norfolk, whose

ROUTE TWO

family had remained Catholic at the Reformation, gave a vast sum to build a much grander church. An architectural competition was held for designs in the style of the Italian Renaissance; and a young man called Herbert Gribble, newly converted to Catholicism, won. In fact, funds ran out before Gribble's lavish design was complete, and Gribble's twin turrets planned for the front were never built – and the dome was added some years later.

The interior is a riot of color, with altars and statues collected from continental Europe. The marble figures of the twelve apostles were found in an Italian warehouse, having been thrown out of Siena Cathedral. The Lady altar was grabbed in Brescia from the rubble of a church being demolished. The fine altar of St Wilfrid was bought from an impoverished church in Holland, which in turn had obtained in from Rochefort in Belgium.

Today the Brompton Oratory is the church of choice for London's first-rate gentry

THE CENTER OF FASHIONABLE CATHOLICISM, CLOSE TO HARRODS SHOP

of Catholic persuasion – and its the neighborhood is now filled with first-rate shops.

The Oratory church is open daily 6.30-8; tel 020 7589 4811.

CARDINAL NEWMAN, WHO INSPIRED THE CATHOLIC REVIVAL IN VICTORIAN ENGLAND.

ROUTE TWO

Holy Trinity, Brompton
Cottage Place

Lurking behind the huge and ornate stone edifice of the Brompton Oratory is a dull parish church built in white brick, turned gray by London grime. Yet in the present Christian scene Holy Trinity, Brompton — or HTB as it is widely known — is hugely more significant.

The church was consecrated in 1829 to serve a parish that stretched as far west as Earl's Court. Economy and utility, rather than beauty, guided its design. A chancel with marble steps was added in 1879; and six years later a gold mosaic reredos, made in Italy, was installed — a sign that the church had adopted the complex and colorful rituals of Anglo-Catholicism.

Today the church is the center of the most vigorous Evangelical initiative in Britain, which is rapidly spreading to America and other parts of the world. The Alpha course, pioneered here, uses all the tools of modern marketing in order to convey a very strict and uncompromising version of the faith. Church members invite friends and acquaintances to a series of weekly supper parties, which are followed by a presentation; and at the end of the series these friends are invited to

This gloomy building is the center of happy Evangelicalism.

commit themselves to Christ. Thousands have churches have now adopted this method of evangelism.

The Alpha literature claims huge success. But critics, in addition to objecting to the 'fundamentalist' content of the teaching material, suggest that most people attending courses are already church members, and that many converts soon slide away. And a survey commissioned by

ROUTE TWO

the Alpha organization itself showed that at best the course slows the rate of decline of church congregations, rather than causing them to grow.

On a Sunday morning hundreds of people gather here for a feast of modern hymns, to which most clap and wave their hands, and long, rousing sermons. A large screen across the chancel arch shows close-ups of the lead singer or the preacher. Critics have also noted the manifest wealth of many of the worshippers, with expensive cars parked outside; but there are also many students.

The old crypt has been turned into modern meeting halls and a bookshop.

The bookshop is open Mon-Fri 10-5.30. The church is on request; tel 020 7581 8255.

HAPPY WORSHIP IN FULL SWING.

ROUTE TWO

CHELSEA OLD CHURCH
OLD CHURCH STREET, OFF CHEYNE WALK

Although strongly inclined to the priesthood, the young Thomas More felt unable to accept celibacy; and in 1505 he married. He rapidly rose up the political ladder; and he also wrote one of the world's most famous books, *Utopia*, which describes an ideal community living practicing a natural form of religion. In 1525 he was wealthy enough to purchase a large house in Chelsea; Holbein, a frequent visitor, painted a famous portrait of him and his family. Four years later King Henry VIII appointed him Lord Chancellor, the highest political office, and he became even wealthier.

THOMAS MORE, WHO WAS BEHEADED FOR OPPOSING THE REFORMATION.

He rebuilt the south aisle of this church — his parish church — commissioning Holbein to design the capitals of the pillars, each of which symbolizes one of More's offices in church and state. And he installed a tomb for himself, writing his own epitaph. But he opposed the king in his wish to divorce Catherine of Aragon, who had failed to produce a male heir; and he refused to accept the Act of

MORE'S BODY, WITHOUT THE HEAD, IS TO THE RIGHT OF THE ALTAR.

Supremacy, which made the king, rather than the pope, head of the church in England. As a result he was tried and beheaded.

There is some uncertainty as what happened to his remains. His severed head was initially placed on London bridge. It may then have been thrown into the river; or it may be have been purchased by a member of Chelsea church, Margaret Roper, and eventually buried with her in the churchyard; or it may have found its way into the Roper vault in Canterbury – a severed head was found there in 1824. His body was initially buried in the Tower of London, where he was executed, but later was placed in his own tomb.

Most of the church was destroyed by bombing in 1941, and has been rebuilt. But the More chapel and tomb survived. So did many later monuments and furnishings. The altar rails, pulpit and delicate marble font all date from the late c17. The Italian artist Bernini is responsible for the memorial on the north side of the nave to Lady Jane Cheyne, who died in 1669 of epilepsy. Lord Dacre, who inherited More's Chelsea estate, has a splendid Tudor monument.

Sir Hans Sloane, an eminent physician after whom Sloane Square is named, is buried in the churchyard; above him is a

TOMB OF THE PHYSICIAN HANS SLOANE, AFTER WHOM THE SQUARE IS NAMED.

canopy housing a large urn. He donated a set of chained books, the only ones in any London church. A kneeler, embroidered by a member of the congregation, commemorates Pope Adrian IV, the only English pope, who donated the land on which the church is built; another recalls Bartholomew Nutt, who ferried people to the church before there were bridges.

It is open daily 10-1, 2-4; tel 020 7352 7978.

ROUTE TWO

PEACE PAGODA
BATTERSEA PARK

One of the miracles of modern history is that within months of the end of the Second World War friendships and alliances were forming between the two sides. And religious people of all faiths and denominations led this movement of reconciliation.

One of the most powerful gestures of reconciliation was that of a Japanese Buddhist order, the Nipponzan Myohiji, which started building pagodas dedicated to peace in the cities and towns of Japan's erstwhile enemies. Britain has two of these wonderful structures, one of which stands in Battersea Park overlooking the Thames.

It was completed in 1985, and stands over 30 meters high. Its walls are clad in Portland stone, and the timbers supporting its roofs are Canadian Douglas fir; specialist Japanese craftsman made the roof tiles in the traditional manner. The con-

A ZEN SYMBOL OF GLOBAL PEACE.

ROUTE TWO

struction was mainly by monks and nuns belonging to the order.

The four faces of the pagoda have huge reliefs, carved in stone and gilded, showing scenes from the life of the Buddha. The south carving shows the Buddha's birth in the Himalayas. The east carving shows his moment of enlightenment, sitting cross-legged under a tree. The north carving, facing the river, shows him preaching his first sermon. And the west carving shows him dying and passing into nirvana.

Each relief has an inscription written in Japanese. In translation they read respectively: worship and revere the sacred relics of the Buddha; let your inner self be serene; the name Buddha means 'enlightened one'; and be righteous in order that there may be peace.

On a warm Sunday afternoon in summer the grass around the pagoda is covered with children playing, young couples lying in each other's arms, and friends eating picnics and chatting — truly a vision of peace. At dawn, summer and winter, there are just a few young joggers struggling along the nearby path, a handful of older men and women taking their dogs for a walk, and one or two hardy souls sitting cross-legged in front of the pagoda and meditating — another vision of peace.

EACH SIDE SHOWS THE BUDDHA IN A DIFFERENT POSE — IN ONE HE ENTERS NIRVANA.

The park is open daily during daylight hours.

ROUTE TWO

BUDDHAPADIPA TEMPLE
CALONNE ROAD

There is an ancient belief within Buddhism that supreme proficiency in a sport is a means of attaining enlightenment. So that may be the reason why London's main Buddhist temple is barely more than the distance of a lob from Wimbledon's tennis courts.

Yet the site is still rather incongruous. The King and Queen of Thailand decided that London needed a Buddhist temple; and in 1976 they acquired an ordinary suburban house in an ordinary, albeit rather smart, suburban street. The attraction of the house, which is a humdrum example of inter-war suburban architecture, was that it had a very large garden — and that the garden includes a hill. On the top of the hill they built a traditional Thai temple. Presumably it was the first planning application from the monarch that the local council had ever received, and the councilors felt compelled to approve it. The king and queen continue to ensure that five missionary monks, in orange robes, live at the temple, and expound the Buddha's teaching.

The temple has two stories. The top story, which is for silent meditation, has a large and ornate statue of the Buddha, and superb murals depicting scenes from the Buddha's life. The lower story, which is below ground level, has a large hall where acts of worship take place every day, and where the monks preach. The pulpit looks like a large basket, raised high above the floor, on which the preacher sits cross-legged. Members of the congregation sit on chairs, with their hands together and their eyes closed. The ser-

THE EXOTIC ORIENT IN A WIMBLEDON SUBURB.

mons are mainly in Thai, since the temple mainly serves Thai residents in England; but occasionally English is used.

The living room of the suburban house has been converted into a smaller temple; and it contains a smaller statue of the Buddha, to which offerings of fruit, honey and sweets are made. People chat and children play quite freely in this temple. And next to it is a kitchen and communal dining room; so as meal-times approach, there are delicious smells of Thai cuisine.

It is open daily 9-5; tel 020 8946 1357.

THE MEDITATING BUDDHA INVITES YOU TO MEDITATE ...

... AND TO MAKE OFFERINGS OF CAKE AND FRUIT.

ROUTE TWO

St Paul's Church
Covent Garden

Known as 'the actors' church', St Paul's has been connected with the theater since the establishment of the Theatre Royal in nearby Drury Lane in 1663, and the opening of the Covent Garden Theatre (now the Royal Opera House) sixty years later. Its walls are covered with plaques to famous personalities, from Charlie Chaplin to Noel Coward; and it is regularly used for memorial services for actors, directors and playwrights.

In 1631 the Earl of Bedford, who owned much of this part of London, commissioned Inigo Jones to design a square, surrounded by mansions, with a chapel on the western side. But money ran short; so when it came for the church to be built, the earl asked for little more than a barn. Inigo Jones in reply promised him 'the handsomest barn in England.'

Jones designed a huge Tuscan portico

A QUIET HAUNT FOR STRESSED ACTORS — AND WEARY TOURISTS.

ROUTE TWO

facing the square; and he intended this to be the main entrance. But the bishop insisted that the altar be at the east end of the church. So the door was never used – and the portico now serves as stage and backdrop to all kinds of street performances. A new entrance had to be made into the back of the church. This in fact is more pleasing than the portico. The wall is red-orange brick, with the eaves of the vast chalet roof providing a porch. Leading up to it is a wide path through the churchyard, with benches on each side where weary tourists rest.

AN ALTAR WHERE THE ENTRANCE SHOULD HAVE BEEN.

The most distinguished inhabitant of the churchyard is the writer Samuel Butler, who died aged 66 in 1902. The son of a clergyman and grandson of a bishop, he rejected the notion of a God who judges, rewards and punishes; and he regarded belief in such a God as an emotional disease. He was enthusiastic about Darwin's theory of evolution, but came to repudiate the mechanism of natural selection. Instead, he asserted, living beings have a 'Life Force' that causes them to adapt themselves to their environment, and these adaptations are passed on to future generations as unconscious memories. Thus, having spurned one religion, he was trying to create another.

WHERE TURNER, THE PAINTER, AND GILBERT OF GILBERT AND SULLIVAN WERE BAPTIZED.

Buried nearby is the first victim of the great plague of 1665, Margaret Ponteous. The artist Turner and the librettist W.S. Gilbert were baptized in the marble font in the south-west corner of the church.

It is open daily during daylight hours; tel 020 7836 5221.

53

ROUTE TWO

PET CEMETERY

VICTORIA GATE, HYDE PARK

In 1880 the Duchess of Cambridge was overwhelmed with grief at the death of her pet dog. And to assuage her grief her husband the Duke, who was the ranger for Hyde Park, decided to open a pet cemetery; and the remains on the dog were interred, with a solemn religious ceremony.

For the next two decades dogs, cats and caged birds belonging to the aristocracy were buried there. Miniature headstones were erected to commemorate them, and epitaphs composed by the owners were inscribed. Many reflect the widespread popular conviction (which, incidentally, John Wesley supported) that animals, as well as humans, go to heaven.

One epitaph reads: 'I faithfully loved and cared for you living. I think we shall surely meet again.'

Another: 'Sleep, little one, sleep, rest gently thy head – as ever thou didst at my feet – and dream that I am anear.'

Another: 'In loving memory of Puskin, my gentle friend and companion for eleven years – so sadly missed.'

Another, seemingly to a somnolent cat: 'After life's fitful slumber, he sleeps well.'

The popularity of the cemetery, and the small amount of land allocated to it, meant that by 1903 it was full. And from the outset the Duke had put railings around it with a locked gate, so members

ROUTE TWO

of the general public could not share the mourners' sentiments.

The Duke, in fact, had a thorough dislike of the common people enjoying themselves in Hyde Park. He tried to ban young couples from courting there. And in 1883 he resisted demands for refreshments to be served, declaring stoutly in a letter to Queen Victoria's private secretary: 'I consider that these parks are for the enjoyment of fresh air, and are not be turned into tea gardens.'

It can be seen through the railings from Bayswater Road, to the right of Victoria Gate. It is occasionally open to the public; tel 020 7298 2100.

ONLY ROYAL AND ARISTOCRATIC PETS ARE ALLOWED.

ROUTE TWO

RADHA KRISHNA TEMPLE
SOHO SQUARE

The Hare Krishna movement — properly called the International Society for Krishna Consciousness (ISKCON) — is well-known for its groups of young people dressed in saffron robes, dancing in the streets, and chanting 'Hare Krishna, Hare Rama'. These devotees live in communities, where they are required to remain celibate, and rise at 4 each morning to pray.

The movement was founded by Swami Prabhupada, who was born in 1896, came to Britain, and worked for thirty years as a salesman for a pharmaceutical company; in the evenings he translated Hindu scriptures into English. In 1959 he renounced material possessions and family life to become a sannyasin — a holy man. He went to America in 1965, where he gained immediate acceptance amongst the hippies of New York and San Francisco; and he founded ISKCON. In 1968 six American members came on a mission to Britain. They won the support of George Harrison of the Beatles, who helped to record the *Hare Krishna Mantra*; it reached Number 12 in the charts. He also bought for them a country mansion in Hertfordshire.

In addition the movement acquired this property in central London. They have turned the ground floor into a vegetarian restaurant, and the upper floor into a temple. Despite the garish colors, it's a homely and restful place. The windows have been reshaped on the inside in the traditional Hindu form, with a pointed arch. And the glass of each window has been painted with a scene from the love affair of Krishna and Radha, the last of which shows them in erotic embrace. Radha, who became a major figure in medieval Hindu poetry, represents the human devotee, who worships God with unstinting passion.

At one end of the temple is a shrine containing statues of Krishna and Radha, each dressed in a red cloak covered in gold embroidery. At the other end is a statue of Swami Prabhupada, who last visited the temple shortly before he died in 1977; a brass tablet announces that he lives forever. Nearby is a bookcase containing his collected discourses, running into 24 thick volumes.

Swami Prabhupuda appointed eleven gurus to lead the movement after his death. But some went badly astray. The

ROUTE TWO

main guru in Britain started having sex with his disciples; and a jealous male disciple cut off his head with a meat cleaver. But now the movement seems to have settled down.

A DEVOTEE QUIETLY CHANTS KRISHNA'S NAME.

It is open all day every day. The vegetarian restaurant downstairs is open Monday-Saturday.

ROUTE TWO

Swaminarayan Hindu Temple
Brentfield Road, Neasden

Hinduism is a religion of sects. Usually their founder is a charismatic spiritual teacher – a *guru* – who attracts disciples; before his death he appoints a successor, and so the sect continues. One of the most popular sects of recent times began in Gujarat, the late c18, led by Swaminarayan. Known as Santhsa, it built temples – *mandirs* – in many of the cities and towns of north-western India, founded schools, and more recently has initiated various ecological programs.

In the early c20 the sect began to flourish in east Africa amongst the Indian settlers brought there by British colonialists. And in 1950 Indian immigrants founded a small branch in London; in 1970 they converted a redundant church in Islington into a mandir. The expulsion of Indians from Uganda in 1971 hugely boosted the English branch. And the Ugandan Indians prospered in England, so the sect planned a new mandir, in the authentic Indian style. Land was acquired in this bleak area of north London, and the foundation stone was laid in 1991.

An Indian architect, C.B. Sompura, designed it; and thousands of craftsmen in India were employed to carve the marble and white limestone from which it is constructed; and followers in England raised £27 million to cover the costs. The result is stunning, competing in beauty with anything to be found in India itself. The exterior has seven tiered pinnacles topped by golden spires, and five ribbed domes. The interior has intricate ribbons of Italian marble linking columns into arches. There

are several shrines to the Hindu deities, at which cakes and sweetmeats are offered, and statues of the sect's leaders.

Beside the mandir is a huge *haveli* — cultural center — designed by a British architect, Nigel Lane, in traditional Hindu fashion. It is decorated with complex wood carvings in English oak and Burmese teak. It includes and prayer hall and marriage hall, plus a kitchen where delicious vegetarian food is prepared.

Beneath the mandir is a museum of the history and teachings of Hinduism. And across the road is a school that is run by the Santhsa.

On busy weekend mornings the temple swarms with people — and glows with color, as the women dress in their finest saris.

It is open daily 9-6.30; tel 020 8965 2651.

MADE IN INDIA, AND TRANSPORTED TO NORTH LONDON — THE EASTERN SPIRIT COMES WEST.

ROUTE TWO

LONDON CENTRAL MOSQUE
PARK ROAD, ST JOHN'S WOOD

Every other mosque in Britain was founded, and is financed and run, by the local Muslim community. But uniquely the impetus for building this mosque came from the British government; and this impetus pre-dates the huge influx of Muslim immigrants that occurred in the second half of c20. In 1940 Britain, standing alone against Nazi Germany, was eager the win the support of the Muslim world. And as a gesture of solidarity with Islam it purchased this prestigious site on the edge of Regent's Park as the site for a mosque the size of a cathedral. In fact nothing was built during the Second World War; and the government handed over the site to a charitable trust representing the Muslim countries with ambassadors in London.

The trust commissioned a design from an Egyptian architect; but the local planning authorities rejected it as being out of keeping with the surrounding architecture. A competition was then organized, in which architects from throughout the world were invited to submit designs — and a British architect, Sir Frederick Gibbard, won. Work started in 1974.

Although the mosque is traditional in conception, and so would fit quite happily in a Middle Eastern city, it nestles quite comfortably amidst Nash terraces and modern office buildings. And the dome covered in copper, and the slender concrete minaret with a wide gallery at the top, now form a major landmark.

The interior is simple to the point of austerity. The inside of the dome is night

ROUTE TWO

A PIECE OF ARABIA IN
REGENT'S PARK.

by a more elaborate Islamic arch; but this pattern is repeated so many times that the hint at flamboyance is lost.

Beneath the mosque is a basement that includes another large hall, and numerous toilets — designed for squatting in the eastern manner, rather than sitting. To one side of the mosque is a courtyard, around which are residences for the imams (teachers).

Despite its beauty the mosque feels a little lifeless — reflecting perhaps its official origins.

It is open daily 4 am — 10 pm; tel 020 7724 3363.

RISING ABOVE THE SMART REGENCY TERRACES.

blue; and at its base is a ring of blue mosaic decoration, punctuated by small, round windows with blue glass. The main windows on two sides have the traditional pointed arch but with no embellishment; and there are matching blank arches round the other walls. There is no furniture at all, since people sit or kneel on the floor. Each place is defined on the carpet

61

ROUTE TWO

St James's Church
Between Piccadilly and Jermyn Street

William Jermyn developed the neighborhood after the restoration of the monarchy in 1660 for the pleasure-seeking elite; and Jermyn Street soon became notorious for its high-class brothels. But he felt even prostitutes and their clients needed religious solace; so he commissioned Christopher Wren to design a church, which was completed in 1684 - taking its name from the nearby palace, where Prince Charles currently resides.

Religion was always mixed with pleasure here. In Vanbrugh's play *The Relapse* the church is mentioned for the witty conversations among the congregation that

Beneath the traditional organ radical ideas are debated.

The church amongst the brothels.

drown out the sermons. Gillray, renowned for his rude cartoons, is buried here, as is d'Urfrey, who made the standard collection of bawdy songs. The fourth Duke of Queensbury, the father of horse racing, is interred under the altar.

This was the only church that Wren

ROUTE TWO

built on a new site, so he had no earlier foundations to dictate the shape. The proportion of height, width and length is exactly 2:3:4.

Grinling Gibbons designed the font — and appropriately he has Adam and Eve engaging in serious business round the stem. The reredos, also by Gibbons, has falling vegetation; a joyful sunburst was added after the Second World War.

Through much of the c20 the church was known mainly for the fashionable weddings that took place at its altar. But since the 1980s it has become famous as a haven for alternative culture — it publishes a magazine called *Alternatives*. It holds lectures in alternative religion and politics, and it houses a center for alternative healing; there are exhibitions of modern art, and all kinds of unusual concerts and experimental acts of worship. The church's mission statement declares that it 'celebrates human diversity — including spirituality, ethnicity, gender and sexual orientation.'

It thus represents the opposite wing of the modern church from that promoted by Holy Trinity, Brompton. The evangelicalism of Holy Trinity undoubtedly has more adherents within the Christian fold; but the eclectic spirituality of St James's is more in tune with the great mass of people who feel alienated from organized religion. And there lies the paradox of St James's: it is an organization, functioning within the structures of the Church of England, embodying spiritual freedom.

It is open daily 8-7; tel 020 7734 4511.

ELEGANT ARCHES TO MATCH ELEGANT WEDDINGS.

Copyright © 2002 John Hunt Publishing Ltd

Text © 2002 Robert Van de Weyer

Illustrations © 2002 Robert Van de Weyer

ISBN 1-903816-12-2

Designed by Nautilus Design (UK) Ltd

All rights reserved. Except for brief quotations in critical articles or reviews, no part of this book may be reproduced in any manner without prior written permission from the publishers.

Write to:

John Hunt Publishing Ltd

46A West Street

Alresford

Hampshire SO24 9AU

UK

The rights of Robert Van de Weyer. as author of this work have been asserted in accordance with the Copyright, Designs and Patents Act 1988.

A CIP catalogue record for this book is available from the British Library.

Printed in Italy

Visit us on the Web at: www.o-books.net